Cambridge Little Steps 2

Phonics Book
Pamela Bautista

CAMBRIDGE
UNIVERSITY PRESS

Cambridge Little Steps 2

1 Letters: Ss, Tt, Bb

👁 **Look.** 💬 **Say.** ⭕ **Circle.**

Phonemic Awareness: Say: *sad* and *smile*, emphasizing the initial sound. Children imitate your pronunciation and facial expressions. They open their books, identify the letters and illustrations, and repeat *socks, bear, sun, smile, sad,* and *mouse* after you. Finally, they circle only drawings with initial *S*.
Practice: Teach this chant: *Sing a song, Sally.* **Sing a song, Sally. Sing along, sing along, sing with me.** You can then sing the chant using children's names.

3

👁 Look. 💬 Say. ⭕ Trace.

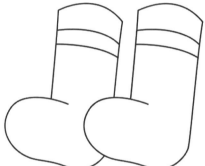

Sound to Symbol: Trace the letters *S* and *s* on the board. Children imitate the tracing using their index finger. Then they open their books and identify the illustrations. They trace the letters *S* and *s*.
Practice: Children use finger paint to fill out a whole sheet of paper with the letters *S* and *s*.

Phonemic Awareness: Say: *Teacher, T-T-T, teacher, tape, table,* and *tree,* emphasizing the initial sound. Children repeat after you. Then they open their books. Say: *The teacher likes the sound T! Color the words with the sound T.* Children identify all the objects and color the *tape, table,* and *tree.*
Practice: Teach this lullaby: *Twinkle, twinkle, little star. How I wonder what you are! Up above the world so high. Like a diamond in the sky.*

5

 Say. Trace. Color.

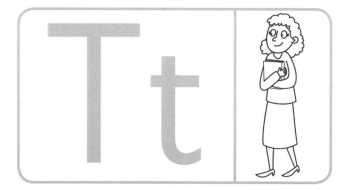

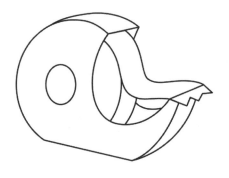

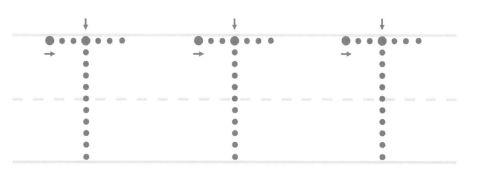

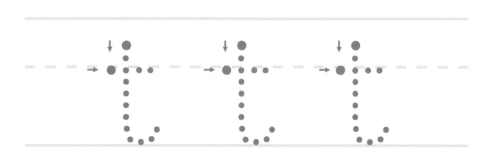

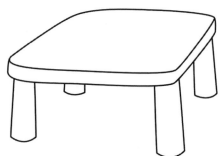

Sound to Symbol: Draw several uppercase *T*s on the board and the same number of lowercase *t*'s. Children draw lines to join uppercase and lowercase *T*. Then they open their books and identify the objects. Children trace the letters and color the drawings.
Practice: Show cards with uppercase *T* and lowercase *t*. Children stand up when they see the uppercase and sit down when they see the lowercase.

👁 Look. 💬 Say. ✖ Cross out.

Phonemic Awareness: Say: *Book, B-B-B, book, bee, bear,* and *bird.* Children repeat after you. Then they open their books. Say: *This book is about animals. All the animals' names start with the B sound, except for one! Cross out the name that is not a B sound.* Children identify the animals and cross out the mouse.
Practice: Teach this chant: ***Baa, baa, black sheep, have you any wool? Yes sir, yes sir, three bags full. One for the master, one for the dame, one for the little boy down the lane.***

7

👁 **Look.** 💬 **Say.** ⭕ **Trace.**

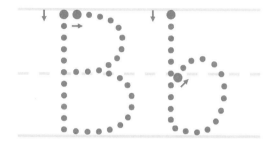 

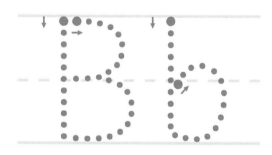 

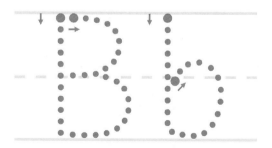 

Sound to Symbol: Show different word cards. Children clap when they see a word starting with the letter *B*. Then they open their books and identify the letters and the names of the illustrations. They trace the letters, identify the words, and trace the arrows, connecting the letter *B* with the *bee, bear,* and *bird*.
Practice: Children use pipe cleaners to create the letter *B*. Half of the group forms uppercase *B*, and the other half lowercase *b*. Then they form pairs of uppercase and lowercase letters.

👁 Look. 💬 Say. ✏ Color.

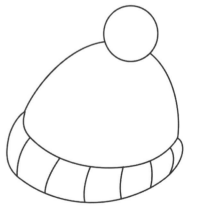

Phonemic Awareness: Say: *House, H-H-H, house, hammer,* and *hat,* emphasizing the initial sound. Children repeat after you. Then they open their books, repeat the words after you, and point at the pictures. Finally, they color only the illustrations with the *H* sound.

Practice: Play *Same or different.* Say pairs of words like these: *mouse-house, hat-cat, hammer-hammer, hook-book.* Children identify whether the words are the *same* or *different.*

🔲 Say. ⭕ Trace. ✖ Cross out.

Sound to Symbol: Trace several uppercase and lowercase letters on the board including several *Hs* and *h's*. Children take turns erasing all the letters except for *Hh*. Then they open their books and identify the letters. Say the words, and children repeat. Finally, they trace the letters, identify the words that do not start with *H (bear* and *tape)*, and cross them out.
Practice: Using your index finger, draw an uppercase or a lowercase letter. Children identify which one it is and say *uppercase or lowercase*.

👁 Look. 💬 Say. ⭕ Circle.

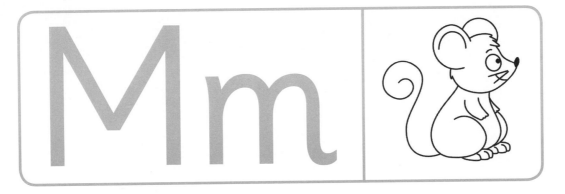

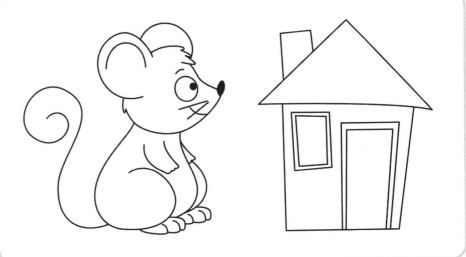

Phonemic Awareness: Say: *Mouse, M-M-M, mouse, moon,* and *monkey,* emphasizing the initial sound. Children repeat after you. Then they open their books and identify the illustrations. They repeat the words after you and point at the pictures. Finally, they circle the illustrations with the initial *M* sound.
Practice: Say groups of three words and ask children to identify the word that has a different initial sound: *moon-mouse-house, monkey-book-moon, teacher-mouse-monkey.*

11

👁 Look. 💬 Say. ⭕ Trace.

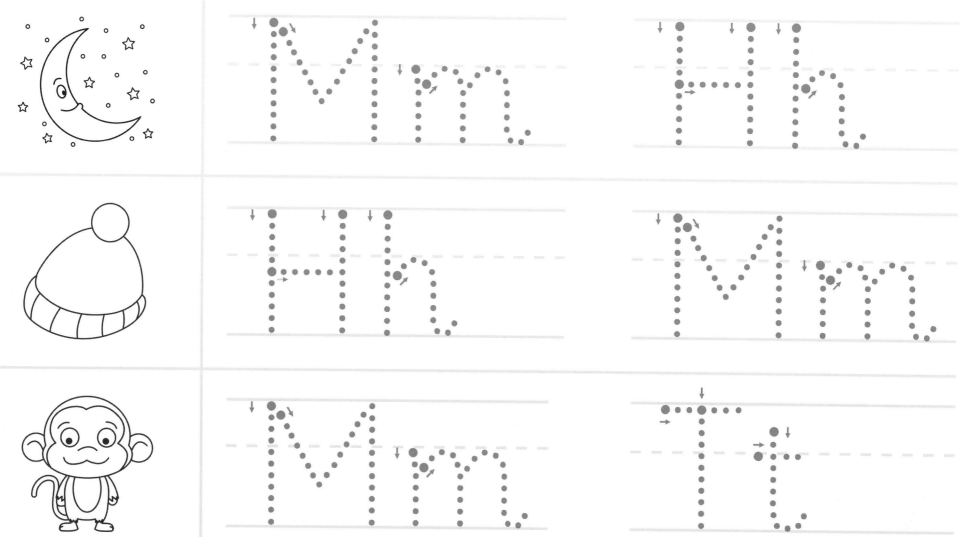

Sound to Symbol: Show a picture of a monkey and say: *Monkey.* Children repeat after you. Show a letter *M*, and children imitate the sound *M*. Then they open their books and identify the name of the illustrations. Finally, they trace the appropriate initial sound.
Practice: Give children cards with an uppercase or lowercase letter from this unit. Play music, and children walk around the room. When the music stops, they find their case partner.

2 Letters: Kk, Jj, Ff, Gg, Ll

👁 Look. 🗨 Say. ✏ Color.

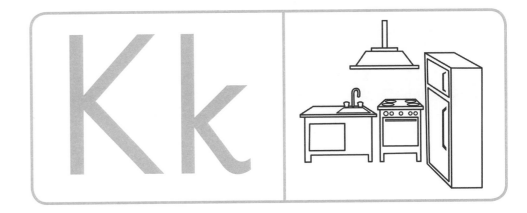

Phonemic Awareness: Say: *Kitchen, K-K-K, kitchen.* Say *koala* and *kettle*, emphasizing the initial sound. Children repeat after you. Then they open their books and identify the illustrations. They repeat after you and point at the pictures. Finally, children color the illustrations that start with the initial K sound.
Practice: Teach this chant: *One, two, three! See Kelly the koala climbing a tree! Climb, Kelly, climb. One, two, three!*

👁 Look. 💬 Say. ⭕ Trace.

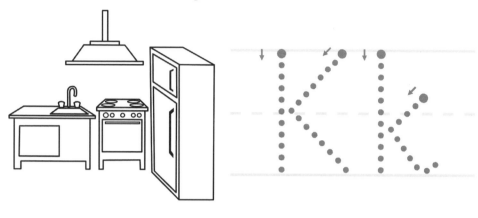

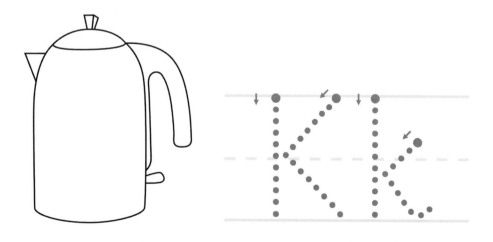

Sound to Symbol: Show the picture of a kitchen and say: *K-K-K, kitchen.* Children repeat after you. Show a letter *K* and say: *K-K-K.* Children imitate the sound. They then open their books, identify the names of the illustrations, and trace the letters *Kk*.

Practice: Using modeling clay, children create uppercase and lowercase letters *K*. Then they identify the case of the letters created by other children.

Look. Say. Draw.

Phonemic Awareness: Say: *Jacket, J-J-J, jacket,* and *jug,* emphasizing the initial sound. Children repeat after you. Then they open their books, identify the words, and draw their own picture of something with the initial *J* sound. Help them by suggesting words they might remember, like *jump, jellyfish, jam,* or *juice.*
Practice: Teach this rhyme: ***Jack and Jill went up the hill to fetch a pail of water. Jack fell down and broke his crown, and Jill came tumbling after.***

15

🔲 Say. ⬭ Trace. ✏ Color.

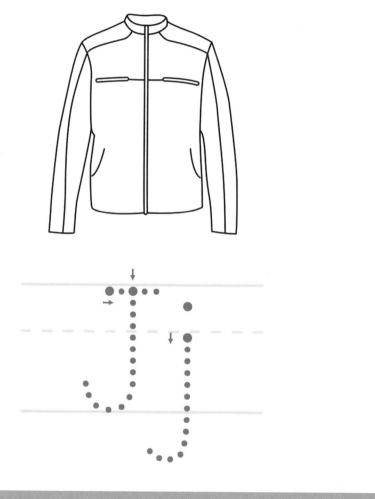

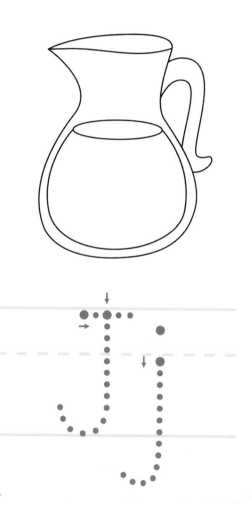

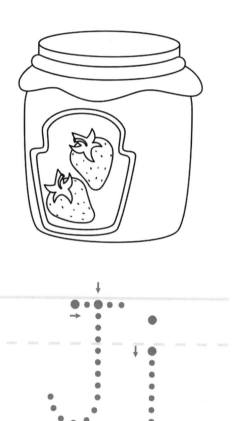

Sound to Symbol: Show flashcards with objects from the previous lessons. Children select pictures beginning with the *J* sound. Then children open their books and identify the letters and the illustrations. Children trace the letters and color the pictures.

Practice: Give children cards with uppercase or lowercase letters. Play a sorting game: *All uppercase jump! All lowercase come to the front!* Finally, ask children to find their case partner.

 **Look.** **Say.** **Color.**

Phonemic Awareness: Say: *Face, F-F-F, face, farm,* and *fish,* emphasizing the initial sound. Children repeat the words. Then they open their books and identify the letters and illustrations. Say: *Face, koala, farm, fish,* and *jacket.* Children repeat after you and color only the pictures that start with the sound *F*.
Practice: Distribute illustrations of objects with the beginning sounds *K, J,* and *F.* Say one of the sounds, and children stand up if it matches the initial sound of their illustration.

17

◼ **Say.** ◌ **Trace.** ✗ **Cross out.**

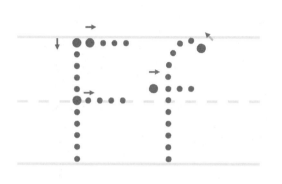

Sound to Symbol: Trace uppercase *F* and lowercase *f* the board and have children imitate the shapes with their index finger. Then have them open their books and identify the letters. Say the words, and children repeat. Children trace the letters, identify the words that do not start with *F*, and cross them out (*jug* and *koala*).
Practice: Give children a piece of sheet with the shapes of the uppercase and lowercase letter *F*. Children glue feathers to fill them in.

👁 Look. 💬 Say. ✏️ Color.

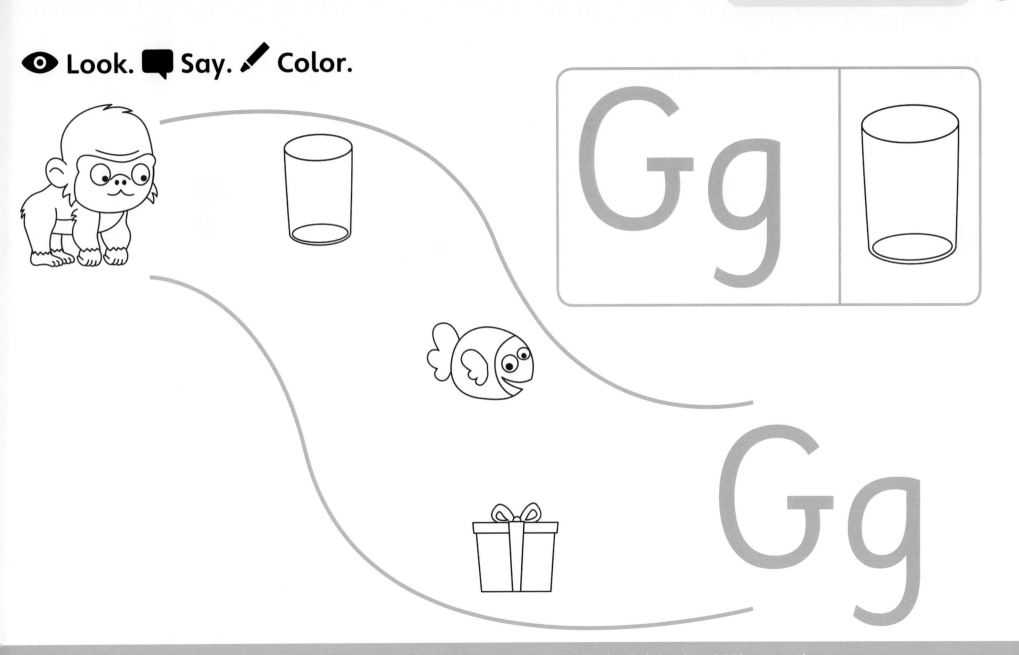

Phonemic Awareness: Say: *Glass, G-G-G, glass, gorilla, and gift*. Children repeat after you. Then they open their books. Say the words, and children repeat after you, pointing at the illustrations. Then say: *The gorilla likes the sound G! Color the words with the sound G*. Children color the *gorilla*, the *glass*, and the *gift*.
Practice: Play *Same or different*. Say these pairs of words: *glass-glass, gift-sift, gold-mold*.

19

 **Say.** **Trace.** **Color.**

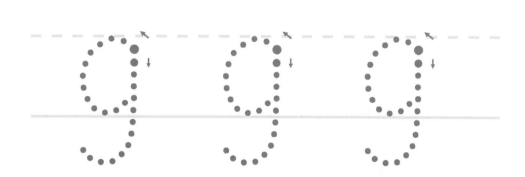

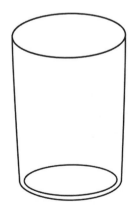

Sound to Symbol: Trace uppercase G and lowercase g, several times, on the board. Children take turns drawing lines matching them. Then children open their books, identify the objects, trace the letters, and color the drawings.

20

Practice: Place the picture of a gorilla next to an uppercase G and the picture of a glass next to a lowercase g. Show cards with G and g. Children mimic the gorilla or drinking from a glass, depending on what's on the card.

👁 **Look.** 💬 **Say.** ⭕ **Circle.**

Phonemic Awareness: Say: *Lunchbox, L-L-L, lunchbox.* Emphasize the initial sound. Say *lemon* and *lion.* Children repeat after you. Then they open their books, identify the illustrations, and repeat after you, pointing at the pictures. Finally, children circle the illustrations that have the initial *L* sound.
Practice: Say groups of three words and ask children to identify the word that has a different initial sound: *lemon-lamb-gift, farm-lion-lamp, lemon-jam-lunchbox.*

21

👁 Look. 💬 Say. ⭕ Trace.

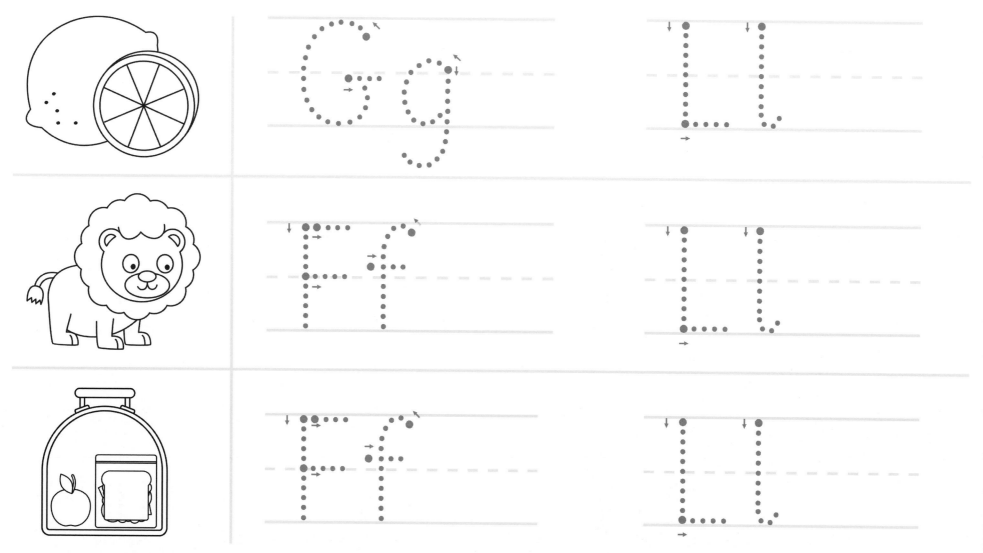

Sound to Symbol: Show pictures of different objects, and children clap when they see an object starting with the letter *L*. Then children open their books, identify the names of the illustrations, and trace the appropriate initial sound.

Practice: Give children cards with letters from this unit, some uppercase and some lowercase. Play music, and have children walk around the room. When the music stops, give an instruction: *All uppercase letters come to the front! All lowercase letters start jumping! Find your partner!*

3 Letters: Dd, Nn, Ww, Cc, Rr

🔲 Say. 👁 Look. ✏ Draw.

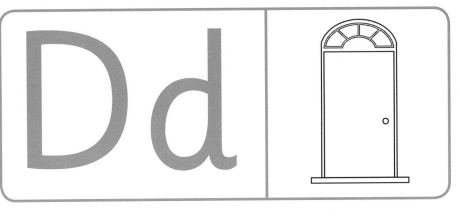

Dd

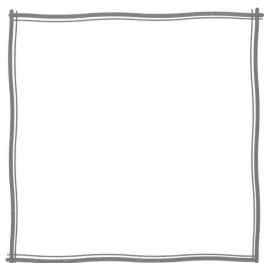

Phonemic Awareness: Say: *Door, D-D-D, door, dress,* and *doctor,* and have children repeat after you. Then they open their books and repeat the words after you, pointing at the pictures. Finally, they draw an object that starts with the letter *D.* Help them by suggesting words they will be familiar with, like *dog, dinosaur, daisy,* and *duck.*
Practice: Say two words, and children repeat only the word with the initial *D* sound: *deer-fear, tress-dress, dance-lance.*

👁 **Look.** 💬 **Say.** ⭕ **Trace.**

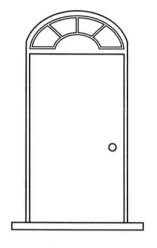

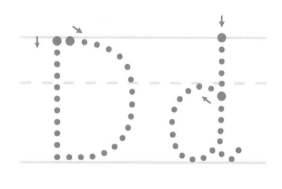

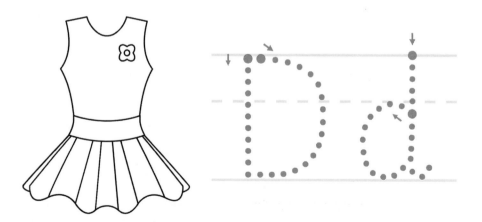

Sound to Symbol: *Show the picture of a door. Children repeat after you. Show a letter D, and children imitate the sound of it. Then children open their books, identify the name of the illustrations, and trace the letters Dd.*

Practice: *Show a variety of cards with uppercase and lowercase letters. Children clap when they see an uppercase letter, and they snap their fingers when they see a lowercase letter.*

 **Say.** ✏ **Color.** ✖ **Cross out.**

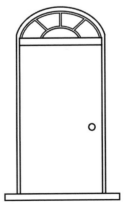

Phonemic Awareness: Say: *Neck, N-N-N, neck, necklace,* and *nose,* emphasizing the initial sound. Children repeat after you. Then they open their books, identify the letters and illustrations, color the words that have an initial *N,* and cross out the ones that don't (*door*).
Practice: Say pairs of words, and children identify whether they are the *same* or *different: neck-deck, necklace-necklace, nose-toes.*

25

◼ Say. ◯ Trace. ✏ Draw.

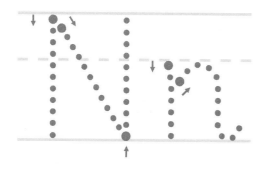

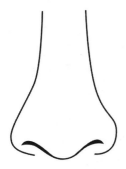

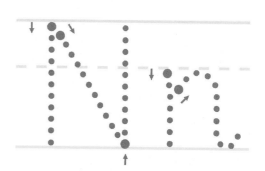

Sound to Symbol: Show different flashcards with objects from previous lessons. Children choose those with the beginning *N* sound. Then they open their books, identify the letters and illustrations, and trace the letters. They identify the words beginning with *N* and draw lines connecting the letters *Nn* with the *nose, necklace,* and *neck.*
Practice: Trace the letters *N* and *n* on the board. Then trace them for children using only your index finger. The children identify whether you are tracing an uppercase or a lowercase *N*.

👁 Look. 💬 Say. ✏ Color.

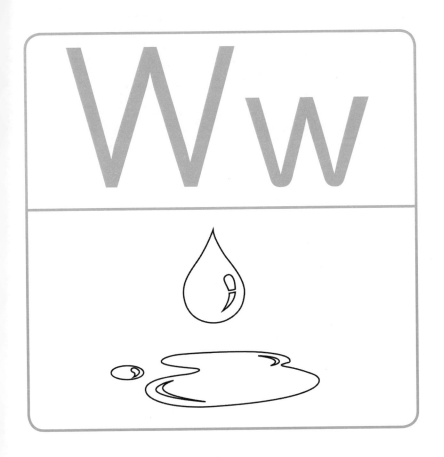

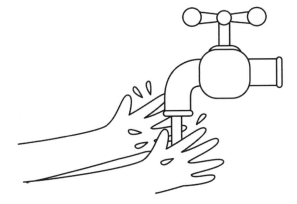

Phonemic Awareness: Say: *Water*, *W-W-W*, *water*, *wash*, and *watch*, emphasizing the initial sound. Children repeat after you. Then they open their books and identify the letters and illustrations. They color only the drawings that start with the sound *W*.
Practice: Distribute illustrations of objects with the beginning sounds *D*, *N*, and *W*. Say one of the sounds, and children stand up if it matches the initial sound of the illustration they have.

⬛ Say. ⬭ Trace. ✖ Cross out.

Sound to Symbol: Show flashcards depicting the *W* words. Children practice identifying and pronouncing them. Trace several uppercase and lowercase *Ds*, *Ns*, and *Ws* on the board. Children draw a circle around the letters *W*. They open their books, identify the letters and pictures, trace the letters, and cross out words that do not start with *W* (*neck*, *doctor*).
Practice: Give children modeling clay. Have them make two long worms out of it. Then they shape the worms into an uppercase and lowercase *W*.

 **Look.** **Say.** **Circle.**

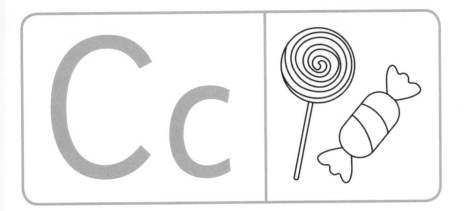

Phonemic Awareness: Say: *Candy, K-K-K, candy, corn,* and *camera,* and have children repeat after you. Then they open their books and identify the illustrations. Say: *The cat likes the sound* K. *Circle the words with the sound* K! Children circle the *candy, corn,* and *camera.*
Practice: Teach the nursery rhyme *The Cat and the Fiddle:* **Hey, diddle, diddle. The cat and the fiddle. The cow jumped over the moon. And the dish ran away with the spoon!**

29

🔲 Say. ⭕ Trace. ✏️ Color.

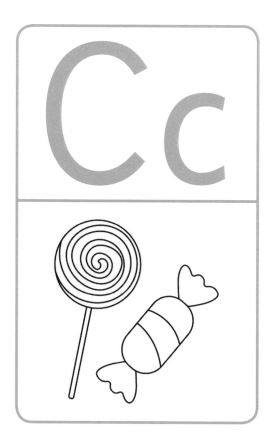

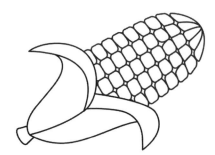

Sound to Symbol: Show children word cards, model the pronunciation, and have children repeat. Then show the word cards again, and children identify the ones with initial C. Then children open their books, identify the objects, trace the letters, and color the drawings.

Practice: Give children a sheet of white paper and finger paint. Children fill the page with letters C, both uppercase and lowercase.

👁 **Look.** 💬 **Say.** ⭕ **Circle.**

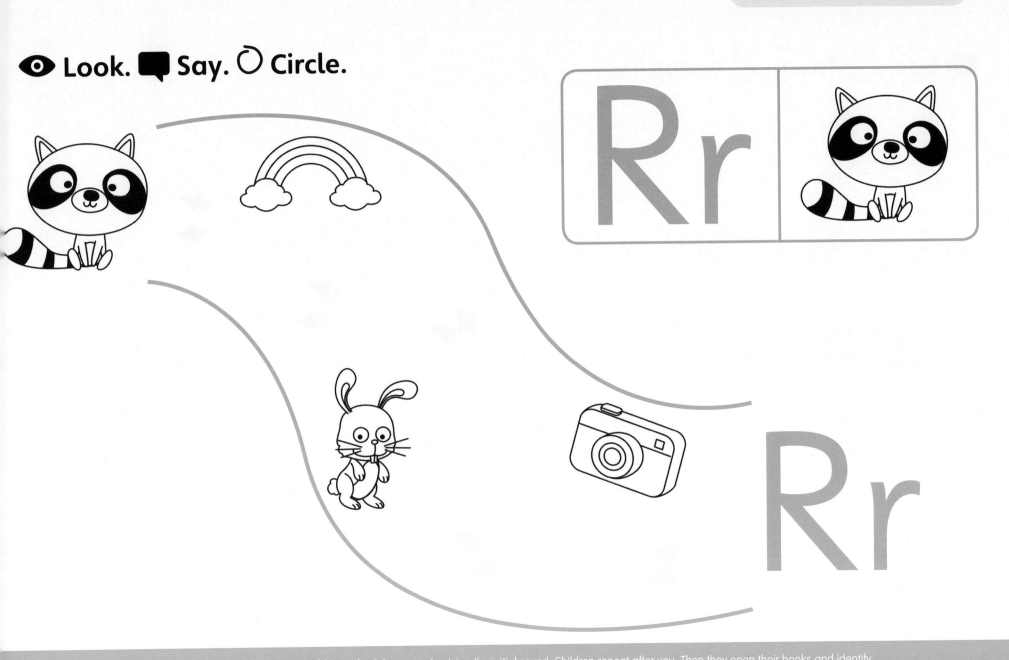

Phonemic Awareness: Say: *Raccoon, R-R-R, raccoon, rabbit,* and *rainbow,* emphasizing the initial sound. Children repeat after you. Then they open their books and identify the illustrations. Say: *The raccoon likes the sound R. Circle the words with the sound R.* Children circle the *rainbow* and the *rabbit.*
Practice: Say words from this unit and ask children to jump forward when they hear the initial *R* sound and jump backward when they don't hear that initial sound.

31

🔲 Say. ⭕ Trace. ✏️ Color.

Sound to Symbol: Trace several uppercase and lowercase letters *Rr* on the board. Children take turns drawing lines matching them. Then they open their books, identify the objects, and trace the letters corresponding to the initial sound. Finally, they color the drawings.

Practice: Give children cards with an uppercase or lowercase letter from this unit. Play music, and have children walk around the room. Stop the music and give them an instruction: *Uppercase letters come to the front! Lowercase letters start jumping! Find your partner!*

4 Letters: Pp, Qq, Vv, Yy, Xx, Zz

👁 Look. 💬 Say. ✏ Color.

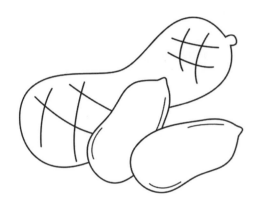

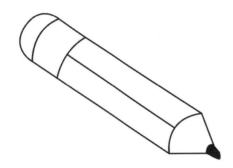

Phonemic Awareness: Say: *Plant, P-P-P, plant, pencil,* and *peanut,* emphasizing the initial sound. Children repeat after you. Then they open their books and identify the letters and illustrations. Finally, children color only the drawings that start with the sound *P.*
Practice: Teach children this hand-clapping game: *Pat-a-cake, pat-a-cake, baker's man! Bake me a cake as fast as you can. Pat it, and roll it, and mark it with P!*

33

👁 Look. 💬 Say. ⬭ Trace.

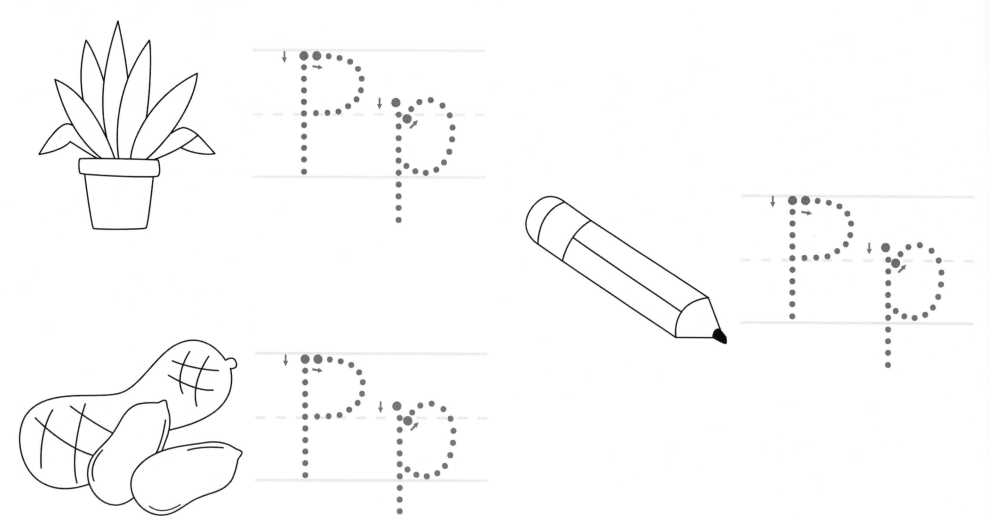

Sound to Symbol: Show a picture of a plant and say: *Plant.* Children repeat after you. Show a letter *P*, and children imitate the sound of it. Then children open their books and identify the name of the illustrations. Finally, children trace the letters *Pp*.

Practice: Give children long and short pipe cleaners. Children shape them to form the uppercase and lowercase letters *Pp*.

👁 Look. 💬 Say. ⭕ Circle.

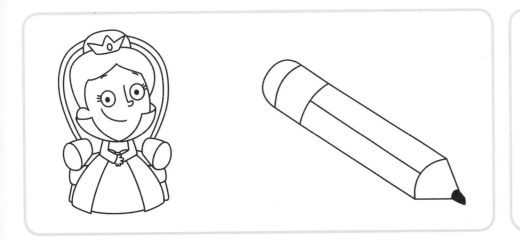

Phonemic Awareness: Say: *Quack!* Q-Q-Q, *quack*, and *queen*, emphasizing the initial sound. Children repeat after you. Then they open their books, identify the illustrations, and repeat the words after you, while pointing at the pictures. Finally, children circle the illustrations with the initial Q sound.
Practice: Say groups of three words and ask children to identify the word that has a different initial sound: *quill-quack-plant, ruler-queen-quick, quill-worm-quack.*

35

 Say. Trace. Draw.

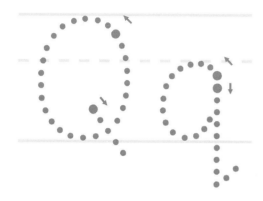

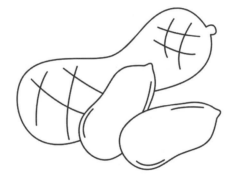

Sound to Symbol: Show different flashcards with objects from this unit. Children select those beginning with the Q sound. Then they open their books, identify the illustrations, trace the letters, identify the words starting with Q, and draw lines connecting Qq with the *queen* and *Quack!*

Practice: Trace the letters Q and q on the board. Then trace them for children using only your index finger. Children identify whether you are tracing an uppercase or a lowercase Q.

👁 Look. 💬 Say. ✏ Color.

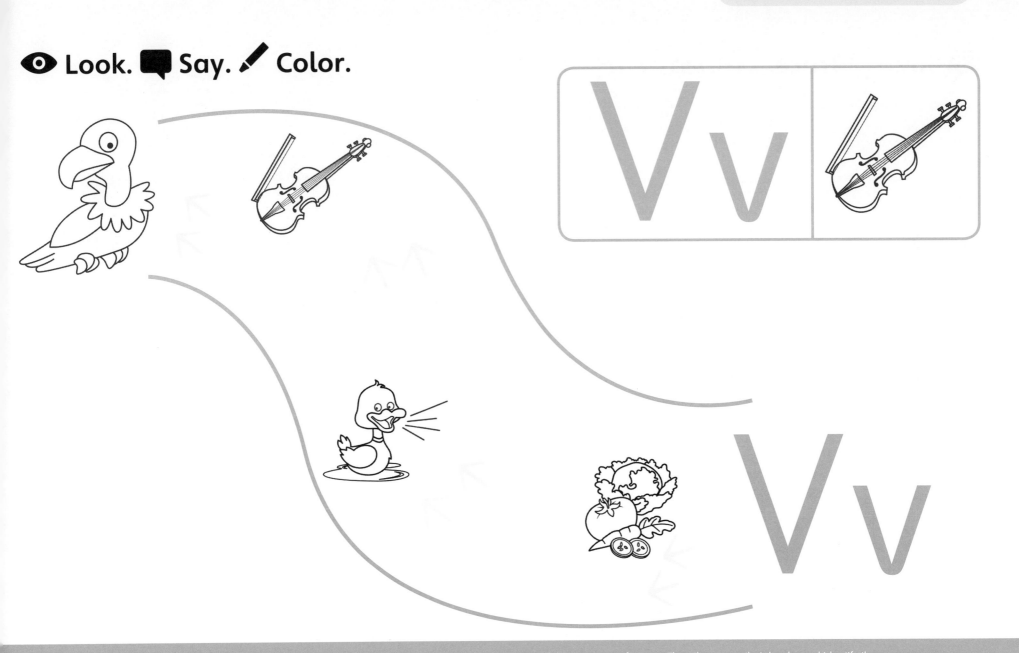

Phonemic Awareness: Say: *Violin, V-V-V, violin, vulture,* and *vegetables,* emphasizing the initial sound. Children repeat after you. Then they open their books and identify the illustrations. Say: *The vulture likes the sound* V. *Color the words beginning with the sound* V*!* Children color the *vulture,* the *violin,* and the *vegetables.*
Practice: Distribute illustrations of objects with the initial sounds *P, Q,* and *V.* Say one of the sounds. Children raise their hands if it matches the initial sound of the illustration they have.

🔲 Say. ⭕ Trace. ✖ Cross out.

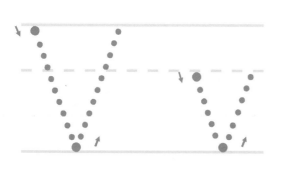

Sound to Symbol: Show flashcards depicting *V* words. Children practice identifying and saying the words. Trace several uppercase and lowercase letters *P, Q,* and *V* on the board. In turns, children draw a circle around the letters *V*. Then they open their books, repeat the words after you, identify the letters and trace them. Finally, they identify words that do not start with *V* and cross them out (*quack, plant*).

Practice: Show cards with uppercase and lowercase letters. Children raise their arms when they see an uppercase letter and cross their arms when they see a lowercase letter.

✏️ Color. 💬 Say. ✖ Cross out.

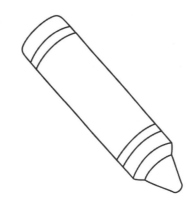

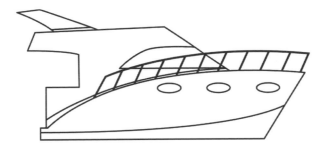

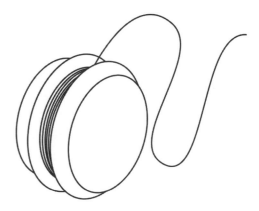

Phonemic Awareness: Say: *Yellow, Y-Y-Y, yellow, yacht,* and *yo-yo,* emphasizing the initial sound. Then they repeat after you. Children open their books. Say: *Color the crayons yellow.* After they've colored both crayons yellow, children repeat the words after you while pointing at the pictures, identify the object without the initial *Y* sound, and cross it out (*violin*). Finally, they color only the pictures of words with the initial *Y* sound.
Practice: Say two words and have children repeat only the word with the initial *Y* sound: *yellow-mellow, yo-yo-mojo, cat-yacht.*

 **Say.** **Color.** **Trace.**

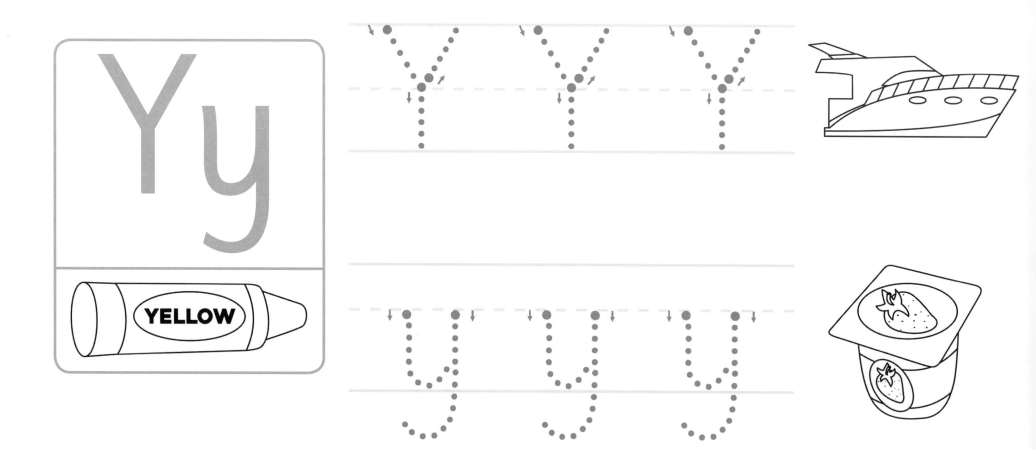

Sound to Symbol: Draw an uppercase Y and a lowercase y on the board. Children stand up and form the uppercase letter with their arms raised. When you point to the letter, they squat without lowering their arms. Then children open their books, identify the name of the illustrations, color the crayon yellow, and trace the letters Yy.
Practice: Give children a sheet of white paper and yellow finger paint. Have them draw as many uppercase and lowercase Ys letter as they can.

👁 **Look.** 💬 **Say.** ⭕ **Trace.**

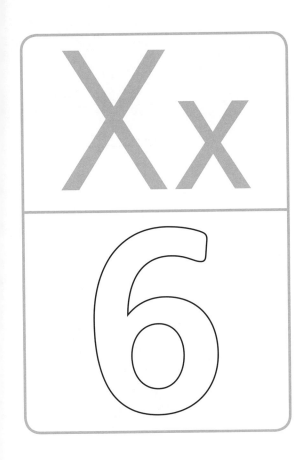

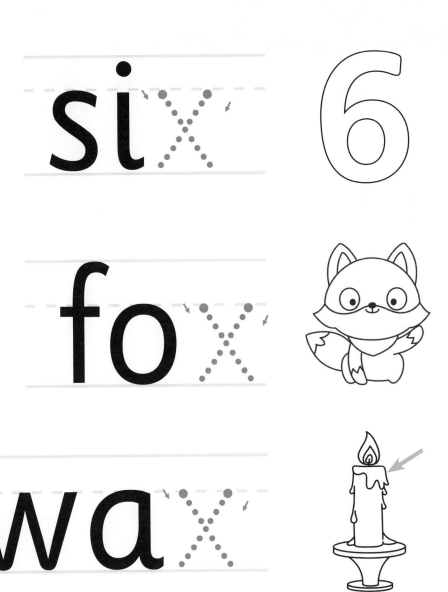

six   6

fox

wax

Phonemic Awareness: Say: *Six, X-X-X, six, fox,* and *wax,* emphasizing the final sound. Children imitate the X sound. Repeat: *Six, fox,* and *wax,* as you show the pictures. Then children open their books and identify the letters, pictures, and words with the sound X. They trace the letter x in *six, fox,* and *wax.*
Practice: Show flashcards with objects from this unit. Children identify the objects by whispering their name. When they see an X word, however, they say the word loudly.

 Say. Trace. Color.

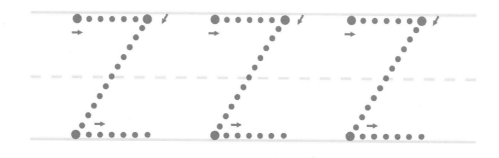

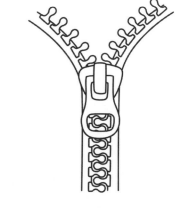

Phonemic Awareness: Say: Zipper, Z-Z-Z, zipper, and zigzag, and have children repeat. Then they open their books and identify the objects. Children trace the letters and color the drawings.
Practice: Give children cards with an uppercase or lowercase letter from this unit. Play music, and have children walk around the room. Then stop the music, and give an instruction: *Uppercase letters quack like a duck! Lowercase letters play the violin! Find your partner!*

42

5

Letter: Aa

👁 Look. 🗨 Say. ✖ Cross out.

Look at this cat!
Her name is Pat.

She's sometimes mad.
She's sometimes sad.
She's sometimes bad!

She chases the rat.
And sleeps on her mat.

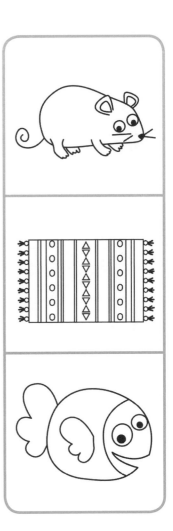

Phonemic Awareness: Say: *Sad, A-A-A, sad, mad,* and *cat, Pat, rat, bad,* and *mat,* emphasizing the middle sound. Children repeat after you. Then they open their books. Read the rhyme, and have children repeat line by line. Finally, children look at the three images on the right and cross out the one that does not have the sound *a* (*fish*).
Practice: Say each line of the rhyme, and ask children to repeat only the last word you say. Then practice the rhyme adding gestures and facial expressions.

 Look. Say. Color.

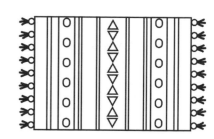

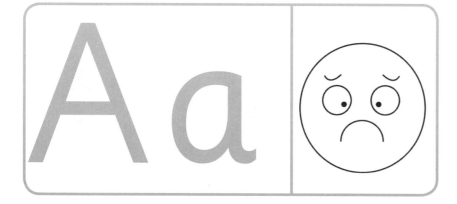

a

Phonograms and Rhyme: Show a card with the letter *a*. Say: *A-A-A*. Children repeat after you. Then they open their books and identify the letter and the short sound *a* in *sad*. They identify the illustrations and color only the ones that rhyme: *cat, rat,* and *mat*.
Practice: Ask: *Does it rhyme?* Say pairs of words, and children identify whether the words rhyme or not: *rat-mat, cat-cake, sad-mad*.

 **Look. Say. Trace.**

s a d

r a t

m a t

Sound to Symbol: Show a picture of a *sad* face, a *rat*, and a *mat*. Children repeat the words after you. Show a letter *a*, and children imitate the short sound *a*.
Then children open their books, identify the names of the illustrations, and trace the letters *a*.
Practice: Using finger paint, children draw a *sad* face and the letter *a*.

45

👁 **Look.** 💬 **Say.** ✏ **Color.**

m a d

b a d

c a t

 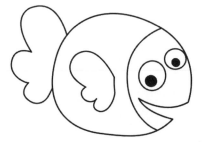

Blending: Write the word *mad* on the board. Show the picture of a *mad cat.* Children repeat the words. Say the word's individual sounds and then say the whole word. Children imitate you. Then they open their books, blend the words, and color the corresponding pictures.
Practice: Give children cards with different letters. They come to the front of the class in trios and form words of three letters each. Children read individual sounds, or repeat them after you, and then put them together to form words.

👁 Look. 💬 Say. ✎ Write.

d a d   P a t

r a t

Blending: Write the letter *R* on the board. Children say: *R-R-R*. Add the letter *a*. Children say: *RA-RA-RA*. Add the letter *t*, and children say: *RAT-RAT-RAT*. Children open their books and blend the letter sounds together. Then they write the words.
Practice: Distribute letter cards *S, A, D, T,* and *R*. Say the sound of each letter, and have children holding that letter stand up. Then say combinations such as *RA, SA,* or *DA*. Help children make groups following your instructions. Finally, children form words from this unit.

47

👁 Look. ☝ Point. 🗨 Say.

1

This is a cat.

2

This is a rat.

3

This is Pat.

4

This is Mat.

Decodable reader: Say pairs of words, and children identify whether the middle sound is the *same* or *different*: *Pat-Pat, cat-Kate, rat-rat, Mat-mate.* Then children open their books and identify the illustrations. Read as they follow along pointing at the words. Finally, children read the sentences by themselves.
Practice: Show pictures of a *cat*, a *rat*, a girl, and a boy. Children help you place them in order as in the reader. Say: *This is…* and children complete the sentence with the words *Pat* and *Mat.* Then say: *This is a…* and children complete the sentence with *cat* and *rat.*

Say. Draw. Trace.

Q q

Z z

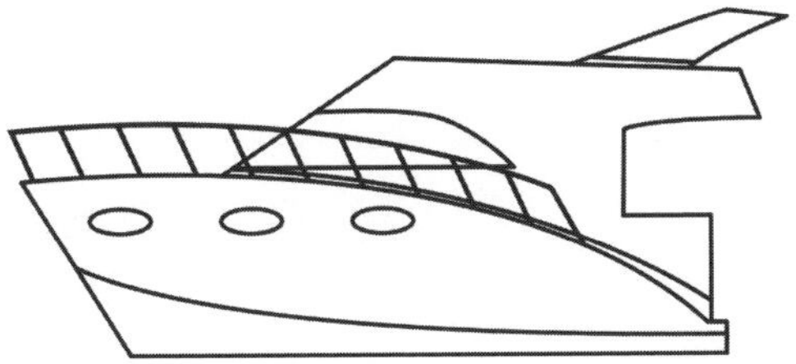

V v

Y y

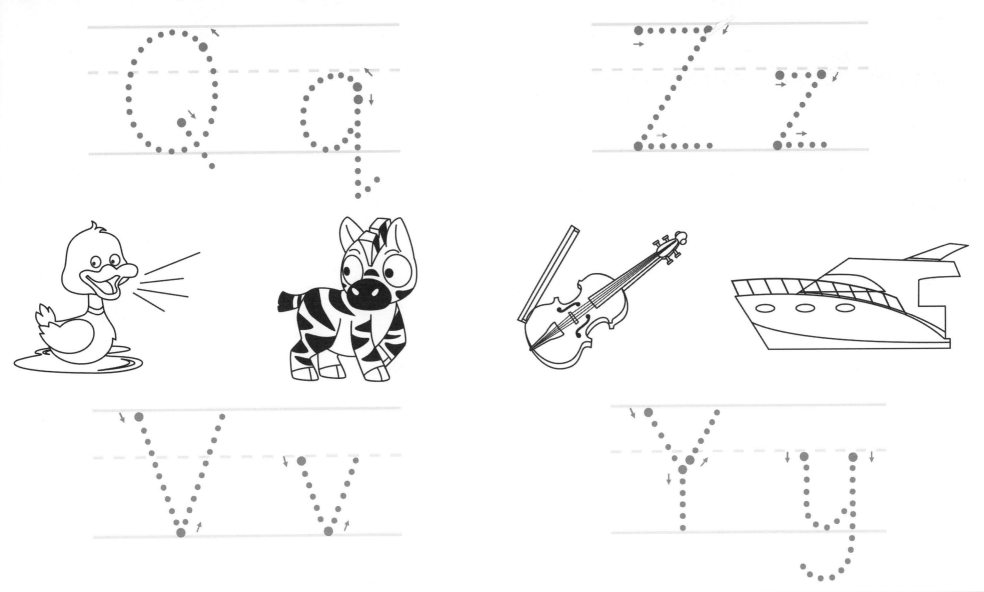

Review: Distribute cards with uppercase and lowercase *Q, V, Y,* and *Z* and pictures of words with these letters. Children find pairs of uppercase and lowercase letters and find the right picture. Then they open their books, identify the pictures, and draw lines connecting them with the corresponding letters. Finally, children trace the letters.
Practice: Place the letters *Q, V, Y,* and *Z* in different corners of the room. Choose some pictures of objects beginning with these letters. Show the pictures, and children walk to the appropriate corner of the room.

6 Letter: Ii

👁 **Look.** 💬 **Say.** ✖ **Cross out.**

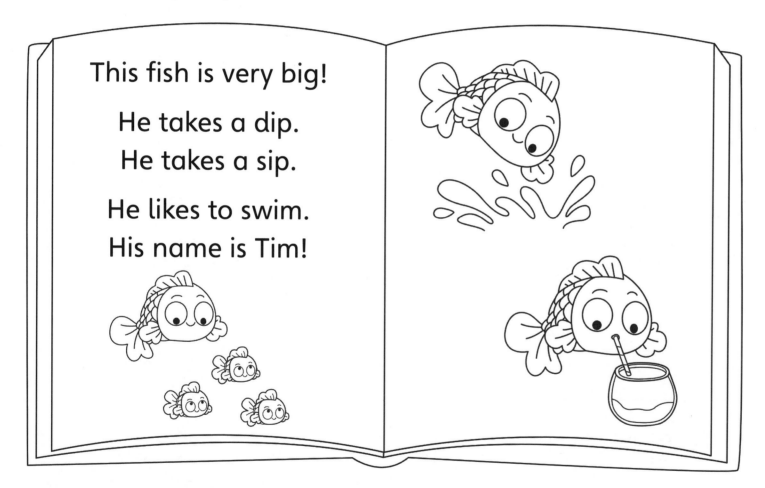

This fish is very big!

He takes a dip.
He takes a sip.

He likes to swim.
His name is Tim!

Phonemic Awareness: Say: *Big, I-I-I, big, dip, sip, Tim, swim, fish,* and *fig,* emphasizing the middle sound. Children repeat after you. Then they open their books. Read the rhyme and have children repeat, line by line, after you. Finally, children look at the three images on the right and cross out the one that does not have the short short *i* sound (*cat*).
Practice: Say each line of the rhyme, and children repeat only the last word you say. Then practice the rhyme adding gestures.

 **Look.** **Say.** **Color.**

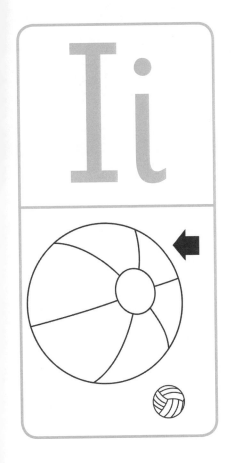

i

Phonograms and Rhyme: Show a card with the letter *i* and say: *I-I-I.* Children repeat after you. Then they open their books and identify the letter and the sound *i*.
They identify the illustrations and color only the ones that rhyme: *dig, wig,* and *big.*
Practice: Ask: *Does it rhyme?* Say pairs of words, and have children identify whether the words rhyme: *big-wig, lip-lap, sit-fit.*

51

👁 Look. 💬 Say. ⭕ Trace.

f i s h

s i t

w i g

Sound to Symbol: Show a picture of a *fish, a wig,* and a person *sitting.* Say the words: *fish, wig,* and *sit.* Children repeat after you. Show a letter *i,* and children imitate the short sound of it. Then children open their books, identify the name of the illustrations, and trace the letters *i.*
Practice: Using modeling clay, children create a fish and the letter *i.*

52

👁 **Look.** 💬 **Say.** ✏ **Color.**

b i g

l i p

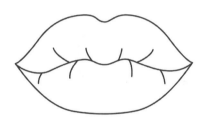

f i g

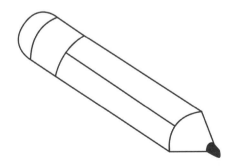

Blending: Write the word *big* on the board. Gesture *big*, in contrast to *small*, and say: *Big*. Children repeat. Say the word's individual sounds and then the whole word again, and children imitate you. Then they open their books, blend the words, name all the pictures, and color only the corresponding ones.

Practice: Give children cards with different letters. Trios form words in the front of the class. Children say the individual sounds and then put them together to form words.

👁 Look. 💬 Say. ✏ Write.

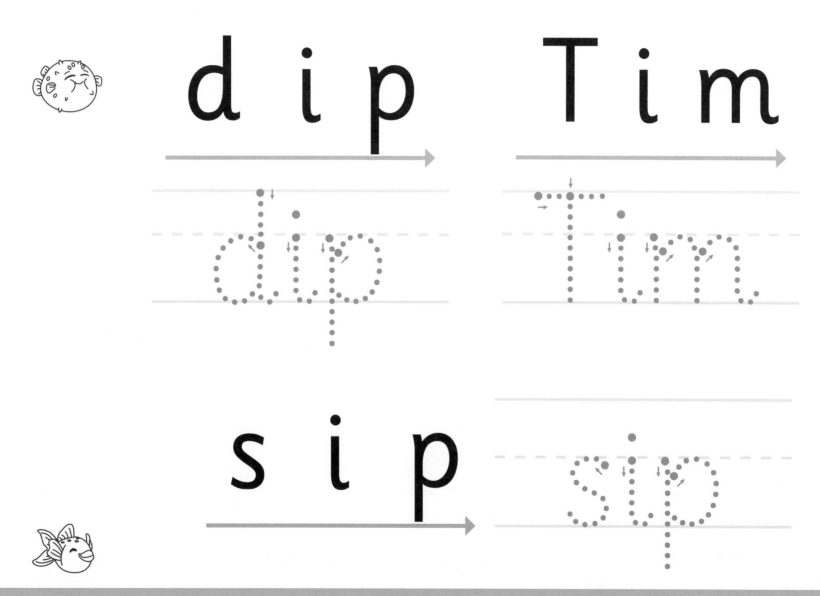

d i p   T i m

s i p

Blending: Write the letter *S* on the board. Children say: *S-S-S*. Add the letter *I*. Children say: *SI-SI-SI*. Add the letter *P*, and children say: *SIP-SIP-SIP*. Illustrate the word by pretending to take a sip from a drink. Children open their books, blend the letter sounds together, and write the words.
Practice: Distribute letter cards *S, I, P, T,* and *R.* Say a sound, and have children with that letter stand up. Then say combinations such as: *RI, SI,* and *TI.* Help children make groups following your instructions. Finally, children form words from this lesson.

👁 **Look.** 👆 **Point.** 🗨 **Say.**

1 Big fish.

2 Big fin.

3 Big lips.

4 It's Tim!

Decodable Reader: Say pairs of words, and have children identify whether the middle sound is the *same* or *different*: *big-big, fin-fine, lip-lip, Tim-time*. Then children open their books and identify the illustrations. Read as children follow along pointing at the words. Then children, with your help, read the sentences.
Practice: Show pictures of a *fish*, a *fin*, and a pair of *lips*. Children help you place them in order as in the reader. Children practice naming the pictures. Finally, say: *Big*, and children complete the phrase with the words *fish, fin,* and *lips*.

✏️ **Color.** 👁 **Look.** 📕 **Match**

i

a

Review: Say different words with the middle short sounds *a* and *i*. Children stand up and clap when they hear *a* and sit when they hear *i*. Then children open their books and color the letter *a* in black and the letter *i* in pink. Then they match the drawings to the corresponding letters using the same colors.

Practice: Use the words from this unit and the previous one. Say one word, and have children identify the middle sound. Choose a pair of words, and have children identify whether the middle sound is the *same* or *different*.

Letter: Uu

👁 **Look.** 💬 **Say.** ✖ **Cross out.**

Doug the bug
has fun in the sun!

He goes for a run,
and drinks from a mug.
Such fun in the sun!

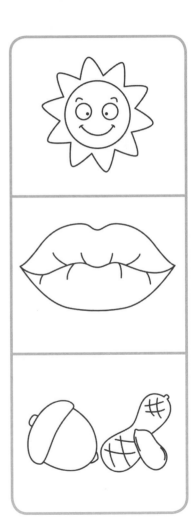

Phonemic Awareness: Say: *Sun, U-U-U, sun, bug, fun, run, mug,* and *nut,* emphasizing the middle sound. Children repeat after you. Then they open their books. Read the rhyme, and have children repeat after you, line by line. Finally, children look at the three images on the right and cross out the one that does not have the short *u* sound (*lips*).
Practice: Say each line of the rhyme, and have children repeat only the last word you say. Then practice the rhyme adding gestures.

 Look. Say. Color.

u

Phonograms and Rhyme: Short u

Phonograms and Rhyme: Show a card with the letter *u*. Say: *U-U-U*. Children repeat after you. Then they open their books and identify the letter and the short *u* sound. They identify the illustrations and color only the ones that rhyme: *hut, nut,* and *cut*.

Practice: Ask: *Does it rhyme?* Say pairs of words, and have children identify whether the words rhyme: *bug-tug, cut-cat, sun-run, bug-big*.

58

👁 **Look.** 💬 **Say.** ◯ **Trace.**

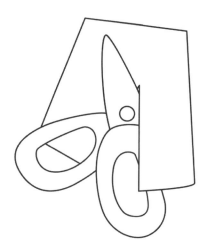

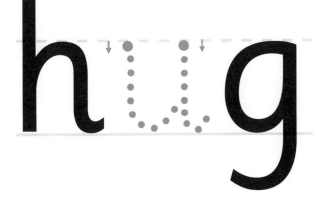

Sound to Symbol: Show pictures representing *hug, cut,* and *sun.* Say the words, and have children repeat after you. Show a letter *u,* and have children imitate the short sound of it. Then children open their books and identify the name of the illustrations. Finally, they trace the letters *u.*
Practice: Using crayons, children color a *sun* and trace several uppercase and lowercase letters *Uu.*

59

👁 Look. 💬 Say. ✏️ Color.

b u g

n u t

m u g

Blending: Write the word *nut* on the board and show a picture. Children repeat the word. Say the word's individual sounds and then say the whole word. Children imitate you blending the sounds. Then they open their books, blend the words, name all the pictures and color only the corresponding ones.
Practice: Give children cards with different letters. Trios form words in the front of the class. Children imitate individual sounds and then put them together to form words.

Look. **Say.** **Write.**

r u n **f u n**

t u g

Blending: Write the letter *F* on the board. Children say: *F-F-F*. Add the letter *U*. Children say: *FU-FU-FU*. Add the letter *N*, and children say: *FUN-FUN-FUN*. Children open their books and blend the letter sounds together. Then they write the words.

Practice: Distribute letter cards, for example, *B, G, T, R, N,* and *U*. Say the sound of each letter, and the children with that letter should stand up. Then say combinations such as *BU, TU,* or *RU*. Help children make groups following your instructions. Finally, children form words from this unit.

👁 Look. 👆 Point. 💬 Say.

1

Bugs run.

2

Bugs hug.

3

Bugs tug.

4

Bugs have fun!

Decodable Reader: Say pairs of words, and have children identify whether the middle sound is the *same* or *different*: *bug-bug, cut-cute, sun-sun, hug-Hugo.* Then they open their books and identify the illustrations. Read as children follow along pointing at the words. Then with your help, they read the sentences.

Practice: Give each child two cards: one with the letter *I* and one with the letter *U.* Say words with these short middle sounds, and children pick the appropriate card.

👁 **Look.** ✏ **Color.** ▮ **Match.**

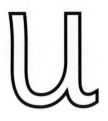

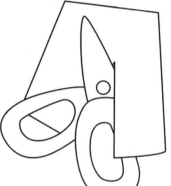

Review: Display the letters *I* and *U* on opposite sides of the classroom. Say words with middle *i* and *u* sounds. Children identify the middle sounds and run to that side of the room. Then they open their books, color the letters in different colors, and match the drawings to the corresponding letters using the same colors.
Practice: Give each child two cards: one with the letter *I* and one with the letter *U*. Say words with these short middle sounds. Children pick the card that matches the sound and show it to the class.

63

8 Letter: Oo

👁 Look. 💬 Say. ✖ Cross out.

Hello, Bob!
Hello, Rob!
Do you like corn on the cob?
Do you play with your dog?
Do you go for a jog?
Tell us, Bob and Rob!

Phonemic Awareness: Say: *Bob, O-O-O, Bob, Rob, cob, dog, jog, mop,* and *fox,* emphasizing the short middle sound. Children repeat after you. Then they open their books. Read the rhyme, and have children repeat it, line by line. Finally, children look at the three images on the right and cross out the one that does not have the sound *o* (*sun*).
Practice: Say each line of the rhyme, and have children repeat only the last word you say. Then practice the rhyme adding gestures.

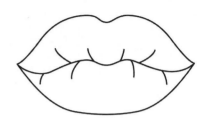

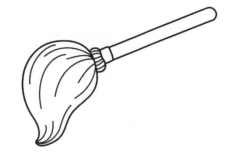

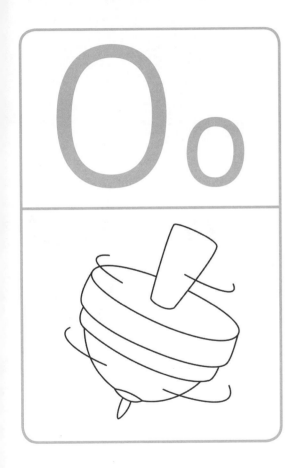

O

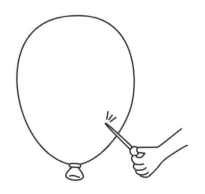

Phonograms and Rhyme: Say: *Top, hop.* Then say: *Top, tap.* Children choose the pair of words that rhymes. Then they open their books, identify the letter and the short sound *o* in *top,* identify the illustrations, and color only the ones that rhyme: *mop, hop,* and *pop.*
Practice: Ask: *Does it rhyme?* Say pairs of words, and have children identify whether the words rhyme: *top-tap, mop-top, pop-pat, hop-hip.*

65

👁 Look. 🔲 Say. ⭕ Trace.

t o p

p o p

r o b

Sound to Symbol: Show pictures representing *top*, *pop*, and *rob*. Say the words, and children repeat after you. Show a letter *o*, and children imitate the short sound of it. Children open their books, identify the name of the illustrations, and trace the letters *o*.

Practice: Using modeling clay, children create a letter *o* and a letter *u*. They press them onto cardboard cards. Play an identification game: Say a word, and children identify whether the middle sound is *o* or *u*.

 Look. Say. Color.

h o p

B o b

m o p

Blending: Write the word *Bob* on the board and show a picture. Children repeat the word. Say the word's individual sounds and then say the whole word.
Children imitate you. Then they open their books, blend the words, name all the pictures, and color only the corresponding ones.
Practice: Give children cards with different letters. Trios form words in the front of the class. Children imitate individual sounds and then put them together to form words.

 👁 Look. 💬 Say. ✏ Write.

d o g   c o b

j o g

 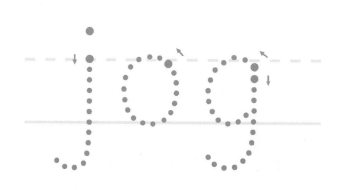 

Blending: Write the letter *C* on the board. Children say: *C-C-C*. Add the letter *O*. Children say: *CO-CO-CO*. Add the letter *B*, and children say: *COB-COB-COB*. Then children open their books and blend the letter sounds together. Finally, they write the words.

Practice: Distribute letter cards—for example, *B, C, P,* and *O*. Say the sound of each letter, and children with that letter stand up. Then say combinations such as *BO, CO,* or *JO*. Help children make pairs following your instructions. Finally, children form words from this unit.

👁 **Look.** 👆 **Point.** 🗨 **Say.**

1

Bob hops.

2

Rob jogs.

3

Bob mops.

4

Rob stops!

Decodable Reader: Say pairs of words, and children identify whether the middle sound is the *same* or *different*: *mop-mop, hop-hope, jog-jog, nod-node*. Then they open their books, identify the illustrations, and point at the words as you read. Then with your help, they read the sentences.

Practice: Show pictures representing *hop, jog, mop,* and *stop*. Children identify the pictures, put them in the order of the reader, and practice naming them. Finally, say *Bob* or *Rob,* and children complete the phrase with the words *hops, jogs, mops,* and *stops*.

👁 Look. 💬 Say. ⭕ Trace.

 s**a**d

 b**i**g

 s**u**n

 t**o**p

Review: Display the letters A, I, U, and O in each corner of the room. Say words with these short middle sounds. Children identify them and run to the appropriate corner. Then they open their books, identify the illustrations, and trace the letters

Practice: Display the letters A, I, U, and O on the board. Form teams and give children four different images. Ask each team to classify them under the right letter, according to their sound.

9

Letter: Ee

👁 **Look.** 🗨 **Say.** ✖ **Cross out.**

Hello, friends!
I'm farmer Ted.
I built a den
for my hens.
Hens lay eggs
in their nests!

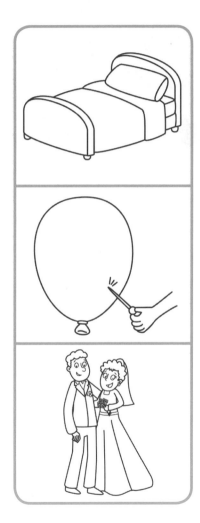

Phonemic Awareness: Say: *Ted, E-E-E, Ted, friend, den, hen, egg, nest, bed,* and *wed,* emphasizing the short middle sound. Children repeat after you. Then they open their books. Read the rhyme, and have children repeat after you, line by line. Finally, children look at the three images on the right and cross out the one that does not have the sound *e* (*pop*).
Practice: Say each line of the rhyme, and have children repeat only the last word you say. Then practice the rhyme adding gestures.

👁 **Look.** 💬 **Say.** ✏ **Color.**

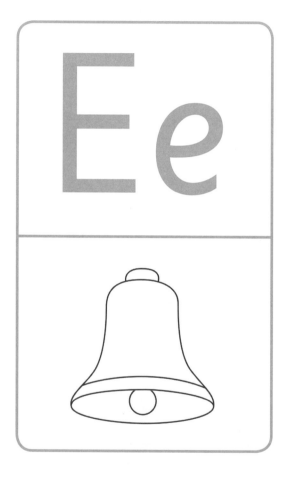

e

Phonograms and Rhyme: Say: *Bell, fell.* Then say: *Yell, fox.* Children choose the pair of words that rhymes. Then they open their books, identify the letter and the short sound *e* in *bell.* They identify the illustrations and color only the ones that rhyme: *bell, yell,* and *fell.*

Practice: Ask: *Does it rhyme?* Say pairs of words, and have identify whether the words rhyme: *fell-fall, yell-tell, bell-ball.*

🗨 Say. ✏ Color. ⭕ Trace.

b e d

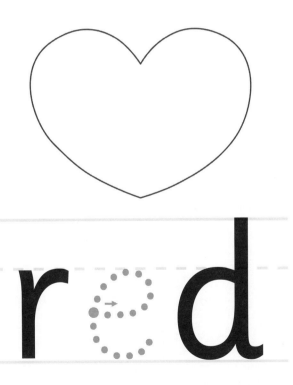

r e d

l e g

Sound to Symbol: Show pictures representing *bed*, *red*, and *leg*. Say the words, and have children repeat after you. Show a letter *e*, and have children imitate the short sound of it. Then children open their books, identify the illustrations, color the heart red, and trace the letters *e*.
Practice: Using pipe cleaners, children create a letter *e* and a letter *o*. Play an identification game: Say a word, and children identify whether the middle sound is *e* or *o*.

👁 Look. 💬 Say. ✏ Color.

b e ll ➝

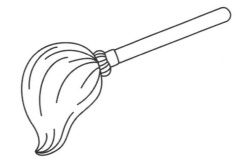

l e g ➝

y e ll ➝

Blending: Write the word *bell* on the board and show a picture. Children repeat the word. Say the word's individual sounds and then say the whole word. Children imitate you. Then they open their books, blend the words, name all the pictures, and color only the corresponding ones.

Practice: Give children cards with different letters. Trios form words in the front of the class. Children imitate individual sounds and then put them together to form words.

👁 **Look.** 💬 **Say.** ✏ **Write.**

w e d   h e n

f e d

Blending: Write the letter *f* on the board. Children say: *F-F-F.* Add the letter *e.* Children say: *FE-FE-FE.* Add the letter *d,* and children say *FED-FED-FED.* Children open their books and blend the letter sounds together. Then they write the words.

Practice: Distribute letter cards—for example, *F, S, L, D,* and *E.* Say the sound of each letter, and have children with that letter stand up. Then say combinations such as *SE* or *FE.* Help children make pairs following your instructions. Finally, children form words from this unit.

 Point. Color. Say.

1  A pet hen.	**2**  A red hen.
3  A fed hen.	**4**  A wet hen!

Decodable Reader: Say pairs of words, and have children identify whether the middle sound is the *same* or *different*: *red-Ted, fed-fade, pet-met, wet-wait*. Then they open their books, identify the illustrations, and point at the words as you read. They color the red hen with the correct color and, with your help, read the sentences themselves.

Practice: Show pictures representing *pet, red, fed,* and *wet*. Children identify the pictures and put them in the order of the reader. Then they practice naming the pictures and finally, with your help, reconstruct the sentences from the reader using the pictures as prompts.

👁 **Look.** 💬 **Say.** ⭕ **Trace.**

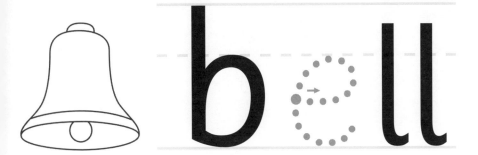

b e l l

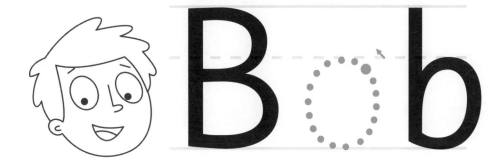

B o b

c u t

w i g

Review: Display the letters *E, I, U,* and *O* in each corner of the room. Say words with these middle sounds. Children identify them and run to the appropriate corner. Then they open their books, identify the illustrations, and trace the letters.
Practice: Display the letters *E, I, U,* and *O* on the board. Form teams and give children four different images. Ask each team to classify them under the right letter, according to their sound.

77

👁 **Look.** 💬 **Say.**

Aa 	Gg 	Mm 	Ss 	Yy 
Bb	Hh 	Nn 	Tt 	Zz 
Cc	Ii 	Oo 	Uu 	
Dd	Jj 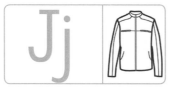	Pp 	Vv 	
Ee	Kk 	Qq 	Ww 	
Ff	Ll 	Rr 	Xx 	

Practice: Invite children to recall as many of these words as they can.

✂ Cut. 🖐 Make.

A	B	C	D
E	F	G	H
I	J	K	L
M	N	O	P
Q	R	S	T
U	V	W	X
Y	Z		

Practice: Use these letter cutouts to play sorting and spelling games with children. Hand out the cards and have children form teams of vowels and consonants, or call out letters to form teams.

79

✂ Cut. ✋ Make.

a	b	c	d
e	f	g	h
i	j	k	l
m	n	o	p
q	r	s	t
u	v	w	x
y	z		

Practice: Use these letter cutouts to play sorting and spelling games with children. You can also mix uppercase and lowercase letter cutouts for sorting games, or to have children spell out people's names or names of cities and countries.